BEING
HERE

JONATHAN IAN ELLIOTT

ISBN: 978-1-963569-79-7

Elliott. Jonathan

Edited by: Barbara Henn and Amy Ashby

Cover design: Daffodils are one of the first flowers to bloom at the end of winter,
announcing the beginning of spring and signifying the end of cold, dark days.
Historically, they are symbolic of strength, resilience and new beginnings.

Published by WARREN Publishing
Charlotte, NC
www.warrenpublishing.net
Printed in the United States

Warren
publishing

*I dedicate this book to Barbara Henn
and my wife, Kate Elliott.*

Barbara was there for me from the first day when I returned to writing poetry after a near thirty-year layoff. As an educator, she was, and has been, as encouraging as she was honest regarding the quality of my work. And in those early days, admittedly, the quality just wasn't there, although I had published poetry in the early seventies in the Virginia Commonwealth University literary magazine as well as several times in a small New York magazine that paid a small sum per poem and several copies each time.

Barbara reviewed and edited give or take a thousand of the three thousand poems I wrote during my most productive days in the Cornelius/Davidson, North Carolina area.

My wife, Kate Elliott, has suffered through reading most of those thousand poems over the past ten years. Her commentary has been both searing and uplifting. But I can always count on her to tell me what she thinks. She does.

I leave it to the readers of *Being Here* to determine if I've provided them with quality verse.

A Mother's Hand
(Through the Worst of Times)

As I've grown old, I've learned to deal with grief as best I can.
Vision limits what I see, and time corrects my memories.

And magic happens less.

We think we leave the dirt roads of poverty of our past,
the worn-out clothes, the whistle of the wind through
the clapboard sides.

The uncertainty of train trips back to Virginia from that
West Virginia coal mining town, as we had done so many times.

I was four, then five, then seven, and again. My mother,
twenty to twenty-three back then.

She squeezed my hand to let me know all would be alright,
though it hardly ever was.

She taught me to believe that something was going to change;
it hardly ever did.

Like an old screen door, no matter how many times it's opened,
the spring slams it shut.

As I sat by her bedside when she was eighty-nine, she squeezed
my hand again, and like before, we knew what that meant.

At seventy-six, I choose the lens through which I wish to see.
The touch of a mother's hand.

The magic of that memory.

WHAT "BEING" MEANS

The Beauty of Darkness Sharing Light

I learned early on through my youth and early teens
that where the skies were, that was home.

And all we had to show for it was a pickup truck loaded
with daily laundry, a double and a single bed, a few
utensils, bowls, and plates.

But the night skies guided us from town to town,
beyond the unpaid rents where we had lived.

Head out the window, as a young lad, I stared at the stars
as though they were mine to take in, to nurture me
for the poet I'd become.

I smiled at them.

They were friendlier than the days I emerged at new schools,
and the ribbing I would take for who I was: a country boy
with a dialect, a drawl, that caught the other kids off guard.

Friends were as tenuous as waiting for that pickup truck
to show it was time to move on.

The night skies never chided me or gave me pause to believe
I was less than who I was.

Each star a sign of innocence to cheer me on, to say,
"We're here for you for the taking!"

Those stars that guided me to believe in the beauty of darkness
sharing light, those that have carried me through these elderly years.

The Spell of the Mysterious Us

The spell of the mysterious us of those we've loved,
the nourishment of who we've been together,

the shadows of voices past, the rich embodiment
of who we were, are, the toils, the suffering,

the shifts of moods, the regrouping, the blunders
we made, the forgiving, the struggle to make sense of it all.

The sometimes animate, sometimes robotic us.

The sometimes strangely silent, sometimes loudly us.

Estranged or mindfully in sync. The need to recreate
ourselves only to discover it was us all along.

We migrate to our friendships, pair off like geese,
forever bonding, regardless of our fallacies, frailties,
fought into winds and weather we never could have conceived.

We are friends.

Memory and Imagination
(In Memory of a Mentor, Jerome Bruner)

Memory and Imagination,
the fragile balance, the storyteller's evidence:

I have lived among the communal rituals of my
West Virginia clan,

reenactments of my mind, tale-telling who we were,
who they were, back then.

Passing on one's culture, the power of expression
to raise awareness of a world that's passed the here and now.

That speck of humanity, their remoteness, in the universe.
That flow of humanness that will never be with them again.

Restrung, like chords of creation, not lulled by illusion,
but by the crescendo, the fall, in how they lived their lives,
experienced their world.

Their social world, the changes, the fragmentary pieces
that made no sense to them over time, to attempt to improvise
what cannot be improvised.

Bad patches in the patterns of their lives.

The attempts not to be undone, undone.

Even with one who has a way with words, it is a challenge
to tell how that real world really was, our notions of what was real
made to fit ideas of our realities.

It is a matter of faith to tell a tale from memory and be
mercifully aware that fallacies exist.

That's All There Was &
All There Is of Life

If a man has a place to lay his head, he is not impaled by poverty,
but may wish for a bagel, a bit of tea.

And the pleasantry of conversation with someone he adores.
That's all there was all there is of life.

To look around and see nature's work in poetry.
That's all there was & all there is of life.

To see the rainbows of life as the clouds clear.
That's all there was & all there is of life.

I recall the pine tree-covered mountains in my youth
& Coal River overflowing after rain.
That's all there was & all there is of life.

I recall the lioness lying with her three cubs in South
Africa's bush area.

That's all there was & all there is of life.
I've looked up and seen a billion stars on a clear night.
That's all there was & all there is of life.

I have loved and been loved to the point of tears
in my memories and all that gives me what a man needs.

That's all there is of life.

A Land of Maybes

Maybe it was in the third grade when I realized I had
no friends.

Maybe it was because I stared out the window during
class time, only to be chastised by each teacher who ever noticed.

There were those who stared out too. Loners like me.
We were not the social kind, nor felt need be.

Maybe I was King of the Loners Class.

The world outside allowed for imaginations a class never
fathomed, to close my eyes and feel extinct like the dinosaurs.
I had a book on them at home, and one of every extinct fish
that ever was.

Maybe this was just another wilderness, except of concrete
and asphalt, filled with blocks and squared-off roads, people
walking in right angles, street to street, lives driven by the
stoplights that behold them, swarms of them.

Unlike the home I had in the hills of West Virginia
with my kinfolk.

Maybe one day I will go back to West Virginia if only
in my memories.

Maybe I will write poetry then about the bobcats,
rainbow trout, the house where I lived with Mom Tucker,
my grandmother, that house on stilts, where the
snowdrifts were taller than we were. I didn't care.

I am alone here, in only a land of maybes.

Going Nowhere
(My Early Days)

A pulse of wind grows, devours the silence around it.
Evening kills the sun; the horizon buries it.

I think of old friends who chose divergent paths.
Some have passed; others traveled to where
the bright gold gleams.

I chose poetry.
Words over wealth.

My mind travels back toward the past,
returns to times when friends and I shared
laughs and solemn thoughts.

Our vanities, humilities, the real, the surreal—
often the same stories with different twists.

Where are they now?

Their rise from their horizons to new realities,
just beyond the distance,
just beyond the dreams we once knew.

And I chose the path to live where we once lived.
Paddling up the river, backwards,

going nowhere.

On My Way Soon

To go home was a strange incident in those days.
Dad's '50 Ford groaned over the mountain pass.

At last, civilization came into play: gas stations,
convenience stores, folks in ritzy clothes, more
dwellings than I'd ever seen.

Second grade.

I would not do well socially, where the kids mocked
my highland dialect they'd never heard before,
nor I theirs.

We kept our distance, at recess and when
lunchtime came.

But beyond my twang, I out spelled them all
in spelling bees and tests of anything with words.

Being an anomaly, I was no less than a new breed
of creature they'd never seen before.

One to be approached gingerly when they chose to,
given the ragged clothing I wore and unkempt hair.

I was amused by them too.

They were communal kids without relevance to me,
since I believed I would be on my way soon.

And I was.

There for the Taking

The elders of the small white church in Friendly View thought that
God could suppress what a boy's grandmother's switch couldn't do.

At six, the boy was meek, yet occasionally given to rants and raves.
Church folks seemed to think that kids should live among the shadows,
speak only when spoken to.

A preacher said the boy was only a dot on the map of God.

Listening to the women screech in tongues, he screamed too.
Called a little heathen. Soon banished from the sight of God.

The rags he wore and hunger soon gave him imaginings, that
God lived among the starry gloom up yonder between the moon,
darkness, and the edge of night.

Those were the days that launched his love of words, those
pent up tones, those images, that otherwise had no place to go.

Among the strange customs and dialect, how the many widows
voiced themselves, so many of their men lost in the mines.

The pain, the beauty of those women in how they survived.

How could a boy become a man without the words for all of this?
Or wish it wasn't so?

It was.

It was there for a poet's taking.

What Faith Is

As I've grown old,
peace now takes the place of desire.
Serenity sets in on days I don't expect it to.

Outside,
hawks scream with outspread wings and then
they're off again.

Does lie still in shaded woods as though no one can see.

I do.

I am blessed to have lived these many summers here.
The earth has given me the sun and moon, interspersed
with nurturing rain.

Out of the darkness of my life light appears,

and roots begin to surface from broken soil.
I wait for them to take hold and bloom
without retreat.

My mind is so new to think like this.

It's then I wonder if this is what faith is.

The I, My, and Me of My Poetry and Prose

Early on, I lived in my private world of words, imagined
characters as lonely as I was.

Facing unpleasant facts, shouting of those around me, or rage
that could not be spoken aloud, as though I was not around.

The power of the undervalued me to triumph in that world
of make believe. Countless hours, rehearsing love over enmity.

Me, as the subject of curiosity rather than of contempt.
My existence expressed in poetry and prose.

Hoping as I wrote every word to be heard and seen through
a lens of my magical world.

Beyond the slights so commonplace in my youth, as city folks
laughed at my West Virginia dialect until into my teens.

A foreigner, exiled to my room, away from the land of concrete
and masses meandering here and there, tethered to stories
and voices that ennobled the senses, while striving to, if nothing
else, make sense of my world.

Awakened Dreams

The mountain of journeys in his awakened dreams,
testing at times the unexplored, the crags of memories
when awake as unreal as when asleep.

Somber thoughts bred in the remnants of night
when a darkness hovers over him until daybreak.

He cannot sleep.

Moments he feels he will never sleep again.

He is alone among the strangers he knew
back then.

A grandma's switch which lay bare on his skin
like the Devil's torch, the Devil's christening.

Four strokes. Six. The flesh splits slightly on his back.
The scars are washed by the rain that stirs a boy
into the surreal. He is neither here nor there.

He has run.

He has run upon the crags with no place to go.

Grandma takes out the worst the world has laid on her.
Seven kids, a case of syphilis her husband left with her.
She walks hunchback without a cane.

There should be a cane.

She cannot follow him into the rain.
Nor run. She will wait for him.

He has no place to go later on, she knows.
And he grows to recall every aspect of those days,
whether dreams, real or unreal, among the awakening
of all that is surreal.

No sleep aids bring him rest. It is a testament to a boy
who lives in an old man's frame and mind, among the crags,
where the echoes of those mountain journeys still call to him.

The Other Side of His Reality

The boy feels the wound-full presence,
memories.

The writhing pain of flesh.
The father's blows.
The grandmother's lash of a switch.

The angered faces; the twisted lips.

Though he shed no tears—never that—
he feels the whippings.

Dreams, they are his realities.
Day to day.

He drafts his poetry, his salve.

It helps until the balm wears off.
He must produce again.

It is his antidote that dulls the mind.
Soothes.
Mollifies.
He is in his ether for a while.

There are consequences for such memories.
The details. The impoverished feelings
of worthlessness.

He chooses his words microscopically.
Drives him mad at times.

Chooses his view of the universe openly.
He is less than an ant in the scheme of things.

Yet, he has friends.
The other side of his reality.

Alone

The boy aspired to write poetry, prose.
To be a poet before he knew what a poet was.

Prose at seven, poetry in his early teens—
the mind's duress exposed: what was sublime,
what was agony.

The frailty, the shame of poverty. Only
to disclose, line by line, on the printed page,
words that never saw a day outside his tenements.

He read Poe in mid-teens. And wrote so Poe-fully.
As though he stole the words that came from Poe's lips.

But Poe alone could scribe the words Alone,
like a testament to everything the boy felt and dreamt:

From childhood's hour I have not been
As others saw—I could not bring
My passions from a common spring—
My heart to joy at the same tone—
And all I lov'd—I loved alone ....*

The boy soon learned that poverty crafted few friends.

Pain and misery in a poor man's art ascribe to a higher
fate than love—respect and all its elements.

Thousands of times the boy's mind and pen pled
for respect, and the destiny to arrive at who he was
in the light-giving guidance through his humble frame,

among the reluctant understanding of the human
fate in those childhood hours: that he was among
the nearly invisible guests in the universe,
alone.

* "Alone" by Edgar Alan Poe, circa 1829.

A Real Boy Again

At night in Dry Creek, I travel home in my dreams.
But I don't know where home is.

I never know where home is.

It always changes, always a new foreign place.
Dreaming and waking—one is as real as the other.

I wait for my mother to arrive to take me where
she, I, belong; that time where dreams become
reality, and I am a real boy again.

Insomnia

In the night, the restless life, the reimagining returns.
Memory accelerates till dawn. It is a journey wholly alone.

Children perishing from machine guns
that as a young Marine I had sent to 'Nam;

my mother whacks her butcher knife, breaks through
my bedroom door;

the belt buckle slash against the flesh of a boy
not yet five.

Even times of silence tatter, maim the mind.

The depths they take: I cannot swim or breathe
so easily from there. No remedies; anti-depressants
have the opposite effect.

PTSD at seventy-six, and no fix yet.
It's death's idea for the living.

Moments, the hours, the flesh feels more than words
ever could. The reimagining, the boundaries of the conjuring,
limitless.

But day comes like a loyal lover, embraces me till
my darkest hour.

She will come again. And again.

The Means of His Divinity

She never masked her bruises with powder or veils
of rouge. They were her battle wounds.

Not to show that she had lost, but to show
what the man called husband had done.

The landscape on her face a map for what awaited him, as
dark and certain as God himself had witnessed those days.

In youth she was a student of what violence meant;
as she aged, the lessons learned turned to rage,

beyond what any sixteen-year-old girl would have known
when she married him.

At twenty-four, the only scars that showed were those
of hate, revenge; the imprints on his face (a spike-heeled
shoe), the taste of bleach (only a tad, she said) when
he fell into a stupor now and then.

It was his baptism into his world of godliness.
Divorced, he became a preacher man.

And who wouldn't be from what he'd been through?
The victim of an insane wife, he often said.

He said God had called him to sermonize, a spiritual
awakening, he often said. Yet truth stemmed from the war
with his former spouse.

Indeed, she was the means of his Divinity.

Self-Revelation

I write about myself, this character of words.
Fingers bent; gray hair soon turned white.

Recounting what I repeat to myself, syllable
after syllable in prose and poetry.

But how the spaces of time swell, filling and
emptying what I can recall:

The parts I know by heart, the parts too
splintered to reminisce.

I pen in a last chapter until time to put down
the pen, discarding dreams from what might
have been, until there is no more story to tell.

"What Do You Think of Me Now?"

How much is a man a master of his destiny,
his parents twice-divorced?

A girlfriend he loved so openly whose folks
were against a boy of single parentage.

Yet, more than holidays, he sacrificed his early
campus years to visit her, hiking over mountains,
hours past, until arriving at her school.

"You can't drop out," she exhorted time to time.
"My parents would never allow me to see you then."

But grades have a way of telling stories like no
words ever could.

His father collected him, 1965, in a '58 Buick convertible.

"You'll never amount to anything," this man
called father said.

The words cracked as painfully as the belt
buckle that slashed his skin, and a backhand
that could nearly crack the bones of a young
boy twelve years before.

The wheels of the old Buick rolled on and on.

A young Marine whose fate seem sealed called
on the mother of the girlfriend he'd left behind.

The mother, now divorced, exclaimed, "I thought
you knew … she married her professor," twenty
years her elder, having borne him a child.

And like the old Buick, the years rolled on, until
near his father's death, his father turned to his
son's third wife and said, "You made a man of him."

Just one last slap before the grave.

At sixty-six, the boy-turned-man, counseled
a US president and staff. And mentored forty
young folks from blue-collar, broken homes
to help them on their journeys to fruitful careers.

On the internet, he could see photos of his father's
grave, alone, grass overgrown.

Just when he thought he had forgiven him, he
smiled and asked, "What do you think of me now?"

Magic
(Or, Dr. Reitman's PTSD Diagnosis)

The howl of pain can only be heard by the inhabitants there.
The mystery of a boy in early youth chasing magic to halt the sting
of a violent swing of the man called father then.

To soar outside of all this: the unraveling of all that went on
without memories of that turmoil or grief.

Recluse paths where many a boy ran before.

Retreat uphill among the fields for wandering,
where wildflowers, like gardens, reign,
where the willows call to songbirds to come caroling.
To no avail.

It is hard, settling in an old man's mind to awaken from all this.
No more a young boy tethered to another world,

but a man in his seventies who does his best to master words
to shed the shadows of the past and what is unredeemed.
It is magic, after all.

Through Those Darkened Days

A roughed-up quilt from years of wear cannot warm the boy.
The frays from patches, threadbare, bare holes here and there;
meager heat to warm his restless frame.

The wind sways, wanders in, between the rotted clapboard slats.
The doors, windows, creak throughout the night.

Rest comes only when weariness sets in,
and the dawn loses its power to the dark,

and the moon in lightless plight hides beneath the clouds.
The winter's moon grows dim; the restless boy drifts into sleep,

torn more between dreams of grief, abandonment, and the beauty
of the forest nearby.

The caws of crows from mountain peaks stir in early daylight
hours that startle him.

Long since gone, the crows live on through a poet's pen,
embraced by his remembering the tangles of the heart,
replete with swells of creaking howls and whispers of the wind.

It is a story of a boy whose fortunes, like a heartfelt gift through
the worst of it, came grace from those darkened days,
his enlightenment.

Wildflowers

Wildflowers tucked away alongside the riverbank,
spring floods, rain-swollen, roll over them.

Riverside cliffs show the dark depths, lines,
against their walls, where the rage of the river
has been before.

The mountain emptiness here, as recluse as I am,
accepts me as its guest. This, my special place,
my comings and goings,

a place I hide when my world is full of confusion,
tangles of sorrow to be unwound:
dusk will not solve the depths of grief,
nor will dawn.

It's quiet.
Memories come.

It will take a lifetime of wise words, thoughts,
to unravel them.

A child becomes a man before he can intimate
it all. Even then, the words, the thoughts,
abandon him.

Going Forth

Quiet mystery of a lone boy chasing magic in his youth,
to halt the sting of a violent swing of the man called father then.

To soar outside, the unraveling of that went on before,
sheltered away in the wilderness, on turmoil, no grief.

The crowds of mountains hovering above, like kindred
spirits in solitude. Recluse paths where many a boy
likely ran in the past.

Retreat uphill among the fields for wandering, where
wildflowers, like gardens, reign.

The willows call to song birds, Come caroling!
It is a hard settling of a young boy's awakening
from all this.

No more a young boy tethered in another world,
but a man who does his best to master words.

To describe the dreams that could have been
beyond what was.

To live in peace, tranquility, still healing going forth.

Coevolve

The wind surges through the branches of the dogwood tree,
then delicately whispers, smells of autumn gusts of air.

I witness the trembling leaves, the bending branches,
in their infancy.

The smell, the swell, lingers through my nose and throat.
I can see the sounds and hear the colors intertwine; it
gives me glee to be such a part of it.

Diverge, converge, I am an open circuit to the earth.
Rhythms inhabit my mind.

Sensuous, intimate, that wordless dimension that
infuses me. Awareness unfolds in bloom.

The dogwood and I coevolve in experience; the
depths, the listening to near silence of leaves.

I hone who I am from just moments ago to what
has ascended in me.

Against the Current of Unsightliness

The wind, the sun tugs at the trees, requesting
them to bloom. The cherry orchard grows so
beautifully, each flower in its place,

so orderly.

An old man savors them.
He rests within a window's view of the orchard's path.
He is tired now,

the last man whose world is filled with innocence,
where grace and love have a place, but flicker
now and then.

Where beauty still unveils itself to the world's design;
it bonds in promises.

The old man wipes his sleeve across his reddened eyes
in sudden delight.

Where grace, love, and beauty breed, hope can survive
against the current of unsightliness.

Before Winter Comes

Everyone is wounded now and then,
scars of the heart,
the hearths that burn like kindling in the veins.

The pain that comes, goes.
The pain that never goes away.
The pain that grows.
The void.
The little nicks that won't let go.

To plumb the depths of brokenness.
How does one get undepressed?

Life's full of loose threads and broken
wings that neither stitch us together
nor allow us to fly.

Those times starved of gratitude
that siphon life, leave us stranded,
alone.
What hope, full of grace, can we
arouse beyond an angry self when
we view life in a ruthless world?

The challenges to cherish little pleasures
among our greater woes;
to drown out regretful memories;
unhappy thoughts.

But harvest what we can, wheat from
chaff, before winter comes.

Alive

People walk by, unrecognized; I am one of them.
My world is full of goodbyes. Too many of them,
I bear through threads of tears.

Winter has a way for those remembrances.

My world at its end may be an asterisk somewhere
for an otherwise unappreciated life as time goes on.

So, I warm myself with verses now, a reward for years
of work with words, and storms through bad journeys
I've lived.

I can still dream of suns that rise and clouds that float
by, and the distant mountains where I once came from.

The dragonflies of iridescent reds and greens along
Coal River's edge.

And there I was, fishing pole in hand, taller than me,
in patched-up jeans, black flies so pestering they
drew blood.

It's odd: as an old man, I think back then were the best
days of my life.

I was alive then. I surely was more alive.

Aspiring

I aspire to be more than I am, only
to discover I already am that one,
that one who wishes too much, whose
poetry and prose expose all his frailties.

Respect, the guest who comes to visit
time to time. That invisible other who
comes in and out at will, a self more
likened to lash out at who it is.

It is just one more means of creating,
creating, through the pain and misery
of what was. Rarely and reluctantly
satisfied.

The unbearable duress of sleepless nights,
difficult to remain in rhythm when hope chooses
to hide beneath the sheets and will not reveal
itself again, in the blink of an eye, gone.

When morning comes, the pen is just
an accomplice of a tired mind, free
from the claims of poetry or prose,
leafing through a thousand words,
a phrase. Praying, devotedly, for
something to arise from the dead.

There must be the help of irony,
that somewhere an angel will cast
a spell on a poetless one to create
the morbid, the joyful, the sublime,
in words that uplift beyond the agony
of demons that steal the words from
one's lips and hands.

Limbs of the Willow

The willow is stronger than a man's ravaging, or the rage
of the wind whipping at its limbs.

The beating ceases when the storm depletes itself,
before the boughs give in, before the rain cracks
at its core. A young willow becomes stronger than before.

What storm can resolve to beat these limbs to concede
to its will when they deem so mightily to do otherwise?

Those eerie hours when whipped into such pitch, by every
given measure, the boy thinks, never should have been.

Every limb a switch to the skin the boy endured.
That's what the willow means to him.

That's why the boy ran.

Knowing when the storm is over, he will go back
to what he will, for the meantime, call home.
It will never be a home to him.

Like all the other times, his mother will be waiting,
suitcase in hand for his uncle, or a train ride, or bus,
to carry him to the safety of kin.

As the willow faces storms again and again, he will
return for more, and as the willow in the worst of storms
survives.

The Flesh of the Rose

When in the dark, light will bloom in evidence of love and nurturing,
the rose, empowered by the earth and emerging rain.

What seems like weeping by its bow, it does not grieve.
But from past arid earth it grows beyond exhausted soil,
of its diminishing.

The flesh of the rose is never tethered without pain that roots
beneath the surface, grace and beauty yet uncovered for the
masses to see and love.

What is beaten is not where the magic is in its early signs of grief.
Incomplete, the shape of leaves unknown.

It is what reveals itself when fully grown.

Eating Cereal

The father always eats cereal with his head down, never
noticing the small son who sits across from him, waiting
for his dad to say a word, any word, to him.

A son's curiosity about such things–the silence–
he will learn to imitate. Even the way a dad holds
his spoon,
the bad blood,

the rage his father brings in the evenings, the wild
heartbeats that boil the brain.

The way the child will learn to curse his life, and who
to blame, just like his dad does.

For now, the son will be invisible until the nightly tirade.
The curses in the darkness, indistinguishable words.

The boy will watch his father, spoonful after spoonful,
staring down, and is too young to wonder if his life will
end up like this.

The truth is as blinding as eyes in sunlight.
But it will not be exposed yet.

It will never be exposed until it's too late to eat cereal
any other way.

The Last of Friendly View

The land tells us when it's time to go. The mine
decides when's the time to crash. It murmured
all its warning signs. No one took heed.

The mines, angered at that, inflicted
its wrath upon men who now, like phantoms,
should have known, unstable trembling just
before it chose to kill fifty working men.

Cinders burning amidst their writhing moans
that lingered on until muscle turned to bones, and
the odor expelled.

Waves of anger and fear among the widows
of a deep and darkened land. They would live
out what was left of life for them.

The elderly without children in sight became
clear: this was the last of Friendly View.

The old outhouses still stand, but little more,
while thirteen years have passed.

There used to be flowers in her yard. Irises.

Her favorite flower. Mom Tucker, the lifeblood
of Friendly View.

She said she'd never leave, be buried there.
Too many ghosts. Her youngest came for her.
She left there in her seventies.

The weeds created their community where flowers
used to dwell. And the dark green forest beyond yields
to a few passersby the pungent odor of the pines.

The moon hardly glows beyond the mountaintop.
The land resorts to what it was before the Scots-Irish
began to settle here.

What does it do without its youth, or men to mine, or even widows
to say they'll stay to the end?
The end came.

A Time to Weep

There are times in life we wish we had never met someone,
but know that someone changed who we are.

A man named Murph lay on a bunk, quivered about
silently.

We were 3rd Marines, 3rd Field Service Regiment
who shipped supplies to our guys in 'Nam, fifteen hundred
miles away.

One day I trailed the other guys outside when Murph
surprisingly confided that he was a machine gunner, now
loaded on Thorazine.

The Marine Corps hoped to salvage him. Gunners were
a premium.

He had gunned down four VC, Viet Cong, or so he thought,
only to find he had killed four children. He described what
shots from a machine gun will do to a child, inconceivable.

He knew our group shipped food rations, field gear,
machine guns, and shells.

At eighteen, I began to think of what we sent, and how
they killed children and parents of those who would never
see their children again.

The horrors of war became intimate. Maybe the guns
I sent weren't the ones that killed kids, but killed someone
who had folks back home, waiting for them.

Over the years, there've been times I've put those thoughts
aside. But then see on the news the killing of children in what
some feel is justified as war.

Those days never leave; without warning, sometimes the tears
will stream. If only I'd never met Murph … but I know better now.

Maybe I wanted to believe, at eighteen, I was only doing
what asked to do. But at seventy-five, it feels like something
else, what Murph felt.

Something no anti-depressant, or therapy, ever wipes away.

She Did Not Die Alone

Her daughter flees her mother's room.
Assisted living is no place for the living, her mother says.

Her mother screams violently, cries because she's alive.
"No one should live like this! Not even a dog!"

It is a place filled with canes, crutches, walkers, wheelchairs,
power scooters, mechanical lifts, ventilators, emergency
alert devices, toilet safety rails, durable as advertised:
The Gift of Mobility, All to Meet Your Basic Needs.

Sold reused after several years, sanitized; repaired.
Her daughter buys her senior diapers that she
won't wear.

"I'm not a child!" Her mother says. "I can't sleep in these!"
Caregivers change her underwear, bathe her almost daily.

She forgets at times where the bathroom is, ten feet away.
She then urinates in the trashcan nearby.

The daughter buys her milkshakes. Strawberry. And
French fries on weekends. For those who won't eat
from the four menu offerings, hot dogs are optional.

Her two sons visit occasionally. At times, she believes
the oldest is her husband.

She spends her time carting her two teddy bears up
and down the hallway on her walker's stand.

They like it, she says. They watch TV with her
until it's time for them to go to bed.

The actors' characters on TV are real to her.

It is fitting when she passes, she has her teddy
bears to hug.

She did not die alone.

HUNGER
and
RESPECT

Hunger

Last remnants of the night, the moon recedes.
A stream of stars glimmers in the darkness one last time.

Drips of dreams, imaginings, fade; drips of life lie
in the somber thoughts of a boy. His dreams, realities,
coalesce.

In sleepless nights, he will suppress the will to feel.
He is neither here nor there.

Feeling is not a given thing.

A boy can die before he lives in what the world has given
him to create, recreate, who he is or wants to be before he
becomes a man.

He fears most the night when the moon returns and
the stream of stars glimmers in the darkness once again.

And charity is lost to him.

For Another Night

I search in thirst to find something that will un-strangle
my past to ward off sleepless nights.

The will to be born again, evolve beyond those days
that allure me back.

That mental landscape without form, frail as it comes
and goes, the quest to know what has reduced me to this.

No quill, no mindfulness, will do.

To drink from a stream of detail; I can't help but to be
accurate. Yet, violence in the abstract dries the mind
of all else.

The fleeting bruises, the child's cry; there is no sound.

What seems so long gone, the signs of times past
come again.

And I remember! Oh, God, do I remember!

The light outside, the chirping birds, a sign that this is the end
of it for another night.

For another night.

Hopefulness

A boy sits by the side of the road and waits. This is where
his mother will turn onto the old dirt road to come for him.

She *hopes to see him soon*, she says in letters he gathers
from the general store. There, the post office is another

hopeful place where months have turned to years.
"It's only a matter of time," his Grandma Tucker says

as she gives him change for an RC Cola and PET vanilla
ice cream. He holds the money tightly in his hand.

What does *matter of time* mean? It puzzles him. He sits a while
longer, throwing stones across the road before he goes,

before his grandmother wonders where he is. The store
is nearly a mile away. What happens if his mother comes

before he returns? For the moment, it is a reason
to wait, as though the world is on his side.

Soon Buried by the Night

The poor stare more than the wealthy do.
Eyesights of the deprived, empty, unreadable;
shoulder blades like skeletons.

Life seen like broken mirrors; memories of childhood,
those reminders of what they never became.

Cold, meal-less, exposed in shadows of a night
where men and working girls bathe in the zenith
of the moon.

They are a people in a land without benevolence.
Hushed only by the signs they display that speak
for them:

"Will work for food!"

They never do.

They stand near the grocery store that's near but
seems so far away.

A woman from her car gives one a *five*.

"It's hard work," she says of all of them.
"What normal folk would work like that out here
for the pittance they make?"

She moves on,
        her taillights soon buried by the night.

Sanitized

As a poor boy, I decided I could be anything
I wanted to be, as long as it was only
in my mind.

Black people had signs that showed the way
to *their* restrooms.

Poor white folks went where only *good folks*
were allowed to go, where the *righteous* good
folks only stared at how a kid could look so poor.

Undeniably poor.

And when the kid did his business, no *righteous*
creature would use the same urinal, sink,
where the kid washed his fingers, face.

Because his mother had taught him
the right way to sanitize. To pay no attention
to those *good folks*, and in his mind

to look them in the eye, smile, sanitize them.

A Strange Cry about Nothing

I only grieved when most folks thought it was too late
to grieve, and they wondered why that kid, so strange,

was crying about nothing, when I only cried about hurt
and pain in my own time.

Stealing Enough

A poor woman steals enough cash from her drunken
husband's pants once he passes out.

Now she can afford to take her son on a train to a destination
neither of them want to go,

but does so just the same because the places for them
to go on Earth are running out. They can only go where
the train goes.

The night train has large windows, where a boy can see
the genteel class, where a boy can imagine what life
would be like if he could get off here … or there.

But that's for the imagination.
The somedays.

That may never come.

A Most Important Time

Is this the man I feared as a child? I thought as I walked toward the door.

Slow to answer, he was a shell of the man I knew back then.
Lung and brain cancer ravaged him.
Eyes glazed.

His weak smile told me all I needed to know.
Days were like months, like years to him.

Between breaths he greeted my wife and me.
"How are you ... son?"

Son. A word I seldom heard in my life.

He retreated to his seat, then bade us to come in.
Gangly legs dangling beneath an ottoman.

Shared stares, he and I.

What do we say after these years, each expecting nothing of the other,
each sharing his emptiness of nothing to say?

Maybe another time, another place, we would have made amends.

It was a morning when darkness never left.
The smell of mustiness prevailed.

Soon, he walked toward the bathroom, gone for the hour.
I walked through the hallway to find him, legs hanging over his bed, asleep.
I placed his legs beneath the sheets and brushed the sweat from his head.

It dawned on me; I had never touched my father's face.

We left soon.
A ten-hour drive back home. A few tears here and there.
When I realized, it was one of the most important times in my life.

Poetry without Joy

Some might call it art.
Hatred lyricized in poetry.

The rhythmic sounds of a belt buckle
slash against the flesh.

The boy knows no living without pain,
the muscle that tightens and quivers within.

He is wrong, rather than wronged.
He is hated, rather than hates.
Wronged and hatred will come later.

The sounds of hatred are silenced for now.

A boy turned man can carry wounds for a lifetime,
one internal tear at a time.

In the end, we are all seized by our own madness,
regardless of the past, songs that only one can hear
that would terrify others.

It is a boy-turned-man's painting in rhythmic words.
It is his Goya.
It is his Van Gogh.

One who would grow to write poetry without joy.

Against the Wind

Against the wind endlessly felt like a hurricane.
He was twelve then, five-four, ninety-six pounds.

"Would you like to buy some flower seeds?"
"Would you like to buy some Christmas cards?"
And so he went, door-to-door, selling goods
from coupons he found in comic books to help
his mother pay the rent.

The "no"s lingered on, no one trusting a boy
who showed up at their door, unannounced,
with a show of panic in his voice.

His world would be a world of "no"s, disguised from time
to time by those with looks of worry for the boy, or pity-wise,
but never asking why a boy so thin, with such weakness
in his voice, would be appearing in front of them.

The doors just closed.

A boy like that just grows to be a man, expecting nothing
of anyone, sometimes nor of himself.

It is neither a cruel world, nor one of benevolence.
It is a world with two hundred billion stars in the galaxy.
It is a universe with two billion trillion stars.

In this speck of time and space, there are those who live
their Dickens life and those who close the doors.

The humility of poverty impassive to the masses, a universe
unstirred. Thirty thousand days on Earth, for most no more.

Against the wind, a young boy becomes a man with time
to resolve whether to live in poverty or one to close the door.

A Sight to See

What a poor boy has, that good white folks have,
are eyes.

Eyes to see the maple leaves turn red, packs
of deer running through the woods,
a man standing on the corner with a sign that says,
"Will work for food."

He never does.

He just stands on the corner, never taking time
to watch the maple leaves turn red, the packs
of deer running through the woods.

Just eyes to see himself, and the good white
folks who just
        stare.

CARING

A Place Where Kindness Is

Dreams work to mend the mind in disrepair.
It is where the sleeping garden grows.

Only for the longing, it is where best to come
to know the nature of a rose, where imagination

learns to pluck its weeds. It is a place of ponds
where the whitest lilies dwell. You can swim

there in serenity. Nowhere nearby will you
find a hopeless future there.

Listen to the waterfalls cascade. They will never dry
within you.

It is a place where kindness is.

Don't waste time otherwise. It is your world
to dream as you will, even as the morning
sun shines deep within, even as you
waken to who you want to be.

Even at times when you have trouble listening.

The Days My Mother Seemed at Peace

The days my mother seemed at peace, I came to understand
she was depressed.

The tide had turned on her too many times.
Hands clasped, face toward the floor, she was lost
from the living then. No child in her life for hours to come.

No *I love you* as when her nature was just so.
I picked my times to comfort her.

This was not one of them.

At twelve, I learned the difference between shallow and deep,
what each meant to her and me,

and that depressed by its nature created who we were just then.
I loved her more then.

Felt the suffering so much more than most grown men could.
Felt the guilt of my incompetence to make it right.

A mother who had protected me from violence and the elements.

I could not protect her from herself.
The days I seemed at peace ….

7 Ds

My mother's face is taut and bruised, bright
with dark red marks here and there.

I sit silently, ten years old, waiting like
a good soldier for her next move.

I can see that she is considering our future
again. No more than an hour passes by.

Finally, "Honey, I need you to go to that shoe
store. Get me a pair of 7 Ds; you know what
I like."

Regardless what I choose, she'll say,
"They're just fine." It's always the same.

New shoes, we're off and running again.
Running against a wind that a ten-year-old
boy would think has nothing to do with shoes.

And he'd be wrong.

The Most Beautiful Woman in the World

The bus roared on toward McCrory's One-Day Bargain Basement Sale,
where frenzied women, like warriors, with coupons and cash would battle on.

My mother avoided all that, and stayed upstairs to buy toiletries and her necessities.
She was just excited to have enough petty cash for a few small purchases and the bus
ride there and back.

That day, one-dollar dresses, the special, caused women to scavenge
amid the masses of blouses and dresses, tossed in piles and on the ground.

I bought a white dress among them with large patterned roses, my mother's favorite
flower. She grew teary-eyed, as she had done before when I spent my paper route
cash on her, two years past, when I bought her a bottle of one-buck Evening in Paris
perfume.

It would take me years to understand, that was the last of our shopping out together
in my youth.

She wore the dress one time to show how appreciative she was;
I can't recall her ever bearing the scent of that perfume.

One day, when I was ten, she asked me to go to the shoe store and buy her a pair of
7Ds. "You know what I like, Honey." She depended on me for things like that.

The man at the shoe store teased me, "You must be buying that for a very special girl."

I retorted back, "I'm buying them for the most beautiful woman in the world."

Where Home Is

She waits for the nurse to give her meds.
She has no will, no memory, to take them

on her own. She opens wide by her caretaker's
command. She smiles at the "nice man,"

she calls him. Just when it seems she is
worsening, a speech therapist asks her

questions to which she replies, "I learned
that in the third or fourth grade." As if to say

I will humor you, she answers anyway.
She will walk down the hallway time and again.

No more days of asking, "When can I go home?"
She is settled now. She is one of a klatch

of women her age who dine together each evening.
Who beyond the memory-less days, who beyond

life in their past, know mostly there is now, and
a moniker on their doors that show where home is.

A Kinder Nature

On this lonely hill where I once played,
the old white clapboard house was razed
years ago. In its day, it was even brindled

then, chipped paint and rotting sides.
We climbed beneath the lattices time to time
where occasionally a black snake lay.

Now uncanny silences have settled in where
the boisterous noises of nearly a hundred
children played around these parts decades ago.

The feeling's one of an unending
hush, profound calm, that what was dear
to me so long ago will never return.

Even the wind drones as if it knows it's so.
My thoughts drown in the afterlife of this,
this village that was, the coming and going,

of more what dies than lives. Maybe that's what
becomes of us as we age. But here I hear the
cricket sounds on this day of otherwise idleness.

And I am pleased that life in sweet sorrow sustains
a kinder nature for these little things than it did
for those who thought to dwell here long ago.

Just Be a Friend
(My Tribute to Barbara Henn)

True friend who asked so modestly of me:
"Just be a friend."

We search in life for what we treasure,
filling needs from emptiness to joy.

Mind and heart in sync with what we
hunger for.

There is peace in all of this.

The friendship that rarely asks why.

What is reaped in all of this in absence
and in mystery of why the friendship
succeeds, yes thrives.

It is the sweetness of the charity.
It is what she's sown.

A friend steeped in helping me
un-depress, born into the age
of the elderly, where gray-to-white
ignites the hair progressing day-to-day:

(Call it ripeness.)

She spurs this old emerging poet
to stay attentive to his dreams,
prods him at times to be more than
he thinks he is.

And all the time, he feels so strongly
that she is just so much more of a friend
than he ever deemed imaginable.

More than kind, at times so greatly
more than he deserves.

They Dared to Hope

They dared to hope in hours of stress
beyond the fantasies of youth.

The women made babies for the mines or war
in their village where the angels sang and the old
buried their young.

Life went on.

Aunt Betty planted seeds in Spring;
Uncle Frank worked in the mines.

She sowed seeds for canning beets,
cucumbers, dill, corn, carrots, tomatoes;
whatever else would grow.

She shared with those less fortunate across
the old swing bridge, where landless folks
canned less, had less for winter's curse.

The winters seemed worse from year to year.

The men fished; meat endlessly less plentiful:
the deer dwelled in the highlands beyond
the village hills.

Still, they were hopeful then, hope within their
grasp, akin to believing in Jesus to get them
through those tougher times.

In Spring, with new sprouts came a sign that all
would thrive, and did from year to year.

In time the youth left in their teens, never to return.
The village is a ghost town now, like many mining
towns. But I was privileged to be among these folks,

a child with fewer dreams; I came to divine what hope
was afterward. In memory and in word, I am who I am
because of them.

How Her Love Is Magical

I survive.

In the greater half-life of my years, my hair turning
pepper-gray, then white, like rings around a tree,
I begin to feel many of them.

Concentric days, evening comes, morning once again.
I see the flock of geese fly by; another season gone.

I am a fan of these flying geese, like clockwork flying
where they need be, breath from the air, wings adjusting
orderly, each in turn, rallying into a near-perfect V.

They know who they are.

I am beginning to.

Inwardly, the walls of the world, narrowing. Alone, but
for the grace of a gentle wife, still giving me belief there
is still heart in this world.

I am so grateful for this graceful being. Her light and
presence that sustains, ascending me when descending
seems my reckoning.

I smile at how her love is magical.

Those Who Buoy Us

What has diminished, what have I gained from being old?
Wisdom with some dementia?
Fewer friends to simplify my life?

My outlook for the future (I've lived beyond the age of expectancy)?

Relatives ask how I am; otherwise, I never hear from them.
Prescription lenses change from year-to-year.

Diapers for seniors (by any other name), can't be far behind.
Mother/Father flesh promote TV ads for that smoother Botox look.

Stores of old precious memories, caged away without recall
that they remain.

What's left are friends, mirrors of our minds, who understand
who we are, care less for our differences (we are well beyond
that stage.)

And in that hourglass, time slowly (or quickly) fades; yet, our
intermingling bridges bring light from shadows, sun from rain.

The dissonance reduced.

Still engaging in adventures with those who buoy us.

One of the Lucky Ones

Poor gait, arthritic in her later years, Mom strolled
up and down the hallway from her assisted living room.

She used a walker then with its seat for her two small
teddy bears. She said they spoke to her and often they
sat up on the bed watching TV.

She laughed at repeated Practical Jokers shows,
over and over again.

As savvy as she was, she never used her walker
to walk past the guards where she waved at them
and walked into the parking lot.

It was then she was recaptured and moved back
to the second floor, her room.

It was never home to her, just as no place we ever
lived felt like home to me. But she soldiered on,
her last words to me, "No one should ever have
to live like this!"

At seventy-six, living in a condo for old folks, life
leaning toward the other side, I think of what she said,
and imagine a world of dignity.

Imagining that, I take a nap, snack throughout the day.
The hall is filled with walker-folks. I'm not yet one of them.

I am one of the lucky ones.

Bipolar Madness

In his darkest hours, when a man is lost
and his madness has no name, *

he is destitute of love and family,
born to capricious stents, bouts of sieged despairs.

The taunting ire that burns the mind and flesh.
The otherness of whom he could be,

life in half-hours, changes in temperament.
Searching for the greatest of truths in his
irrational ethos.

The attempts he cannot clarify.
Amusing to some, to the horror of others.

His moon and stars look different than
what others see.

* Bipolar victims often go untreated, and those
  who do seek help often reject the diagnosis.

A Boy Fails to Understand

A boy should understand, he doesn't have what it takes
to become a man.

He is twelve.
He cannot drive.
He cannot shelter his mother, sister, safe and sound.

He cannot make enough to pay the rent.
He tries.

It's 5 a.m.

He arises to deliver morning papers to his regulars.
Some winter mornings, the ice slows him down.
He slides.

Customers want their papers prior to work.
He'll lose them if he's late.

The school day's just something to get through.
His evening route awaits. He'll sell new customers where he can.

He is an old twelve.
He is ill.

He apologizes to his mom for needing surgery.
He apologizes for not having what it takes to become a man.
He apologizes for being who he is.

He fails to understand what poverty is.
No matter that he's twelve, or ill.

His youth is spent wondering why he's failed
in a void where the impoverished must dwell.

How Do We Account for
the Damage Done?

How do we account for the damage done?
Really?

How do we account for the damage done
to the flesh and mind?

The beating. The blood. The bruises.
The ire. The wild-eyed craze that never goes away.
That stare.

How do we account for the damage done?
The child's flesh inflamed. The mean-assed
names that kill the confidence.

How do we account for the damage done
to teens institutionalized for their fury, lashing
out at what?

They don't know. They just know there's
no such thing as love.

They gave in long ago to whom they became.

The pummeling they'll release to anyone
within their power grid.

The beating. The blood. The bruises.
The ire, the wild-eyed craze that never
goes away. That stare.

How do we account for the damage done?

Really?

The Breeding Ground

A boy sits on a barstool among men who curse
their wives. They are likened to a Drunken Good Ole Boys Club.

They see themselves just slight of gods who harness
their wives. They live in that ethos-world of make-believe.

The boy's father is one of them.

The boy urges his father to go. He knows what his
mother is likely to do. But to no avail.

He has school tomorrow, he says.
He's ignored.

His father orders another bourbon and rants on.
The fever pitch has soared among these men.

The boy fears this.
The bar is but a breeding ground for what happens next.

The boy's beginning to learn, a *feast of self*
inflicts many wounds. His mother has mental scars
to show, but scores to settle now and then.

She has never bowed.

The King of Drunken Men passes out at the door.
At five-four, with the help of the boy, she drags him in.

He wakes up, headache too severe, unlike the ones he's had before.

She has peppered his face with a spike-heeled shoe.
"Did you do this?" he asks.
"Honey, you know I wouldn't do that to you!" she says.

Off to work, but he will not go to the Club for weeks.
In the coming months, he will breed more fantasies
about the man he's become.

Running Breathlessly into the Future

A girl teases a boy.
Both are waiting for the school bus to come.

It has snowed, turned slightly to ice.
The boy chases her.

She giggles as the boy strikes a tree limb.
She stops giggling. He is bleeding profusely from his forehead.

Forehead wounds are known to bleed that way.

He runs across the street to where his mother waits,
having heard his screams.

She places a towel around his forehead and tells him
he will have to go to the doctor alone.

His one-year-old sister has scarlet fever, and his mother
must tend to her. He is ten.

He runs to the doctor's office, holding the towel wrapped
around his head.

The doctor says he can do nothing without a note.
He runs back home to where his mother scribbles,
"Take care of my son."

He runs back, and the doctor stitches his head.

The bus and the girl are gone. The towel is nearly soaked red.

He will have many days like this in the future.
Of course, he doesn't know that yet.

He doesn't know that's the way the life of poor folks goes.
No cab fare for the journey he goes on. Only to run breathlessly
into the future.

Experiences Such as This

Two interns and a resident doctor attempt to shock a patient's
heart back into rhythm.

The patient has been in the emergency ward many times,
has the same procedure once again.

A new intern laughs nervously, proclaims,
"I've never seen anyone turn this blue before!"

The resident doctor ignores the remark.
Presses the paddles on the patient's chest until he responds.

Once again, he's brought around. Cognizant.

His wife, outside the small enclave, walks in,
rubs sweat from her husband's head.

An orderly stands with her.

The woman's husband surprises everyone.
"I'm hungry," he says.

She turns to the resident, puzzled by the request.
"If he's hungry, get him something to eat," the resident responds.

She knows what he likes, and goes down the street to a burger joint.
When she's gone, he turns blue again. The orderly stands over him,
screams for the resident.

This time, he's gone.

The woman walks in, small bag of burger and fries in hand.
She weeps, and after hours of form-filling, she leaves, half-broken.

The orderly will go back to school, study his premed slides.

He cannot get the man out of his mind. He will do an about face,
go into the humanities. He will craft his skills. Write poems about
experiences such as this.

The Now of Nothingness

The unpainted house, wood beyond repair, the old porch
that fell in.

It was there my grandmother, hybrid broom in hand, used
it for sweeping and for cracking the back of a naughty boy
who *twice refused to listen.*

She could be kind at times.
But rarely so.

Her option was a switch, broken from a leaf-bare dying oak.
It was the way of mountain folk, not wasting anything.
The oak bore switches for years, the bark used for kindling.

My grandmother was the beginning of the last of them,
those women of coal-faced mountain men who bore sons
who worked the mines and died in the *Great* mine blast.

Child-bearing women?
No more.

Alongside the dirt road, worthless cars stood from years of rust.

Half-covered smokehouses covered in moss, weeds
that grew through old floors.

It is the tale of a poet's reminiscing of the switching,
the sadness, even the pain of what was, of memories
of a place where youngsters made balls from miners'
tape, bats from saplings.

And how the children laughed without dreams for anything.

They fished and swam, and those who dared
jumped from a mountain cliff into the swimming hole.
(The most courageous one died in Vietnam.)

The boy-turned-man went back just once at thirty-five
and wished he never had.

Marjorie Will Know What to Do

It is the time of night to fear him coming in.
Night has emotional states that few have felt.

The backing up and down the project steps,
the crash against the rails. He is drawing near.

He falls inside. The man called father tumbles
to the floor. He tries unsuccessfully to rise.

"Get me the goddamn toilet!" he screams.
The boy exclaims, "I don't know how!"

"Get me the goddamn toilet!" he screams louder.

The boy is ten.

His mother is in the bedroom, protecting
her one-year-old child. She is silent.

"What do you want me to do?" the boy asks.

His father growls. The boy hopes he passes out,
as he usually does.

This time he just rolls about.

The boy will go next door. Marjorie,
the prostitute, will know what to do.
She knows a lot about men.

She opens the door; she's concerned.
She has seen similar scenes play out
before with this man.

She has black specks on her forearms.

She is a bit glassy-eyed.

"It's Dad again." The boy cries.
Half-stuporous, Marjorie rolls her eyes.
She seems to know what to do.

Inside, she screams at him,
"Get off the goddamn floor!"

He listens to her. He always listens to her.

Somehow, like a miracle, he stumbles
about, gets off all fours, then stands,
lumbering toward the commode.

She seems to have become alert
for that moment, a moment the boy
will recall when he's seventy-six.
She becomes almost incoherent again.

Saviors come in all varieties.

I Am Here, I Was Here

I am here,
I was here.
That's all that can be said of this.

Among the many mysteries of who we are.
Or were.

I sensed it would not be an infinite journey,
nor my take on it so popular as to inspire
the masses of those seeking beauty in my words.

I remained a prisoner to myself.

My grief the beginning of my remembrances.
My sorrow for those insane few I loved.

My hunger no more a tyranny than the loss
of self-respect that poverty bestowed on me.

Then how life made such sweet turns.
That life, as I grow old, has led to peace,
tranquility.

No shame in the end,
who I am,
who I was.

The Pirouette

How talented, how resolved, to let the past
be the past, as best she can.

A young girl pirouettes on stage.

She shows all signs of confidence.
Yet the understory has not been told.

She prefers it that way.

She pirouettes again; the audience applauds.
She will take a bow.

She is seventeen, saved by the custody
of the state, saved from a father who abused
her in early youth,

so lecherous.

One would think she would never dance,
never find her place in the humanities, the arts,
                        where culture dwells.

Yet she does so, so gracefully.
For the good folks who cheer.

For what still evolves beneath it all,
that a girl can pirouette her way to life,
poise and dignity.

The past best left as past, unveiled
by one more, one more,
                    and one more bow.

Pulling the Ripcord

Visions cannot be seen, but through the sinews

                felt.

They are the decision-makers

                of who I am,
                what I feel ...

direct me to depression,
        rare joy,   make me cry,
                or otherwise.

Shield me from insanity,
        sanity.   Same process;
                different attitude.

Each has arisen.
Times of suicide,

                that line I've walked
                so gingerly across,
                senses of finality,
                    or not.

Words that are dead before they're said,
because no one cares.
The journey ends anyway; so why not end it NOW!
If morning comes, so be it.

And on it goes, life among the dying feelings. Aloneness.
It's the un-connecting tissue of the chill.

It's the given-in hierarchy of humanness.

And there is always the ripcord   out there.
Those of us who have lived through it, and still *are*
pulled it.

Endlessly Repeated Stories

The endlessly repeated stories we tell ourselves,
to listen and ponder one's own utterances
arising in the end from one's own verse.

Recounting instances of embodiment,
swarms of discourse from one's being.

Lived situations!
Variable and fleeting:

Our loyalty. Our happiness.

The flux of the ordinary *who we are, were.*

Like meandering rivers: all of us to a final
trickle, a final end.

Only the verse or prose leave behind
the vestiges of our charity, compassion,
kindness, or otherwise, or who we wanted to be.

It is a story that only lies on the surface,
floating freely into the ether of who we were.

Into the universe of all who came before.

How Does a Man Un-remember His Past?

How does a man un-remember his past?
The slash of a belt; the whelps of a switch
on his back and sides.

The uncertainties, the habits of abandonment
from those he loved, changing destinies by the year,
or less. Each stay his world seemingly unlike
the one before.

No wizard of words explains the weight of hatred
those broken people possessed; the airs of drunkenness,
insanity that bloomed over the years.

How does a man un-remember his past?

He forgives and then again.

As Long as We Shall Live

As I draw near surgery for the seventh time in life,
more than wondering if this is it, I wish I'd been there
more for my wife:

the trips for work, nightly courses for multiple degrees,
and times my mind was somewhere else.

I was best at that.

And our few friends, our bonds stretch when all
find comfort in families; my wife and I a family of two.

We watch those with grandchildren move anywhere,
do most anything, hours spent to watch those children grow.

They know these are the bonds that need nurturing now.

Old friends still old friends, but less so when it comes
to creating days for play with the little ones.

And that's the way it is,
should be.

And we all have our memories,
for as long as
we shall live.

Grasping What Compassion Was

Winter came.

Dad drank his shots of bourbon in a bar. Ran tabs.
No cash to pay the rent.

Three months, six months passed. The signs of moving on
grew clear before eviction came.

Dad blamed our departing on the cruel hand of management.

The borrowed or stolen trucks marched on.

No internet back then. No one to uncover where we ran,
we vagabonds.

I was schooled as a rule by teachers who spent
more time with me than they would have otherwise.
God bless them all!

Their love of enlightening, my insatiable love to read
(anything), they worked with me until they brought me
into their light of godliness, of sacrifice and zeal.

One might say, "Poor boy!" misreading all the signs.
I learned my art to teach and tutor as their devotee.

They were my mentors for times to come when I would
coach those disposed, those down and out, as they had been.

And to those kind folks who took me under wing, never
to see me again, I grasped, most of all, what compassion was.

Kindly Beings, or Something Less

The indifference of a galaxy turning in the universe;
the seeming flux of a seed to come to be a woman
or man. The laws laid down unknown, leading to

famine or charity;
disease or random elegance;
mind-shadows or epiphanies;
adrift or abilities to rise, ascend.

Those who taste the harvest of alluvial men;
those with dreams or those without imaginings;
those who sing or those drowned out by another's song.

What grows from this, seasons of distress
for the downtrodden? Or the flowering kindness
that weaves eternally?

Worn words of those who feign to aid the helpless
and the old; it is up to tenants of the universe
to take up residence, a community of sojourners,
within our galaxy to choose,

kindly beings, or something less?

To Understand What Godliness Is
(A Poetic Journey over the Years)

I dream before I begin to type, words, phrases,
from endless likelihoods,

the maze of muses I draw from.

To calm, to inspire, to fire the mind, like a slow-moving
waterfall, the words fall into place,

the way they fall ethereally.

Tick. Tock.

In radiant rhythms I pursue, like a grandfather clock that neither
drifts nor changes mood.

Hours on end, I type until it's time for bed.
Then, I dream in quatrains, in restless excess of my mind.

And ghosts, like gods, plot for my next success,
like hymns in their subtlety and grace.

I am not the man I was just a night, nor years, ago.
Humility sets in, and I begin to understand
what godliness is.

If Only Broken Dreams Could Be Mended

The power of pain reveals itself in dreams.
The silent chimes of death toll for those we've loved,
but lost.

When the nightly light has dimmed, I mourn in earnestness.
We relive the dying more than the living in remembrances.

Memory is a cemetery, Charles Wright once said.
The lure of memory, a place where poets dwell.

When I was five and seven, my Aunt Betty took me in
when grandma switched me excessively.

Aunt Betty smoked every chance she got, after every chore.
"They're bad for you," young, full of concern, I once said.

She laughed, puffed out a smoke stream, nearly crossed
the room. Without her chores and cigarettes, she seemed
to have little life at all.

"We'll all go someday," she said. She at sixty-four.

I see her as though it were yesterday. Some nights,
half-awake; sometimes when in my imaginings, I see
her smile at me, yet she seems so sorrowful.

She was so nice in her life, the way she took me in.
No dream should begin or end like this.

If only broken dreams could be mended, I would
give her the life that she deserved, more so than
how she lived.

The Way of Being

A boy, twelve, sees the sea for the first time.
Just as the West Virginia river, the sea has its thoughts.

He learned early on which senses gave him the gateway
to where the fish dwell, the nourishment he needed to survive.

He will learn the immaterial sphere of the sea, outside
its earthliness.

How it speaks, its oral way of life.

Its invisible ether that stirs its visible world.

The swirling air. The way it departs at night
from the day and sun to stars.

Its way of being.

The river rendered many of these things too, less complex,
for the sustenance of Friendly View.

Now the sea is part of the vastness of the world he must
undertake to understand.

It is the vastness of this world outside of Dry Creek
and West Virginia he must undertake to understand.

It is the vastness of this world, even over the decades
he will seek to know it, he will never fully understand.

PEACE
and
SERENITY

We Are Alive!

A gift to us to view in its brief-lasting life.
The murmur of a stream, so innocent,
so serene, so memorable.

How perfect this gift is!
It will not fade today.
Transformed for every moment of our being.

We are still.
That's all it asks of us.

We will remain while the light still glows,
and our passion poses, through our eyes,
our gratitude.

And if not so before, we are alive!

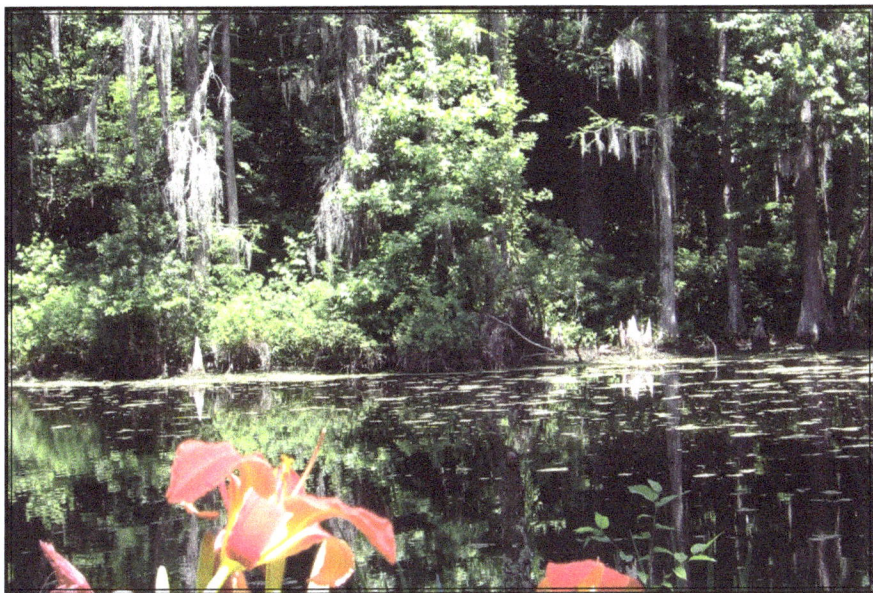

Seclusion

The swamp was my refuge; I breathed in silence, peace; save
the bullfrogs, crickets serenading in their base and alto airs.

The only interludes were two boys who laid their muskrat traps
to sell their pelts; muskrats were abundant there.

Beauty surrounded me, beyond a buckle slash of former days,
or the intense falling out mom and dad displayed. I was ten then.

There was magic in those moments, even some intrigue, the splendor,
and how the flowers grew to add makeup to the scene.

Words have little say in what I felt back then, and how it lifted me.

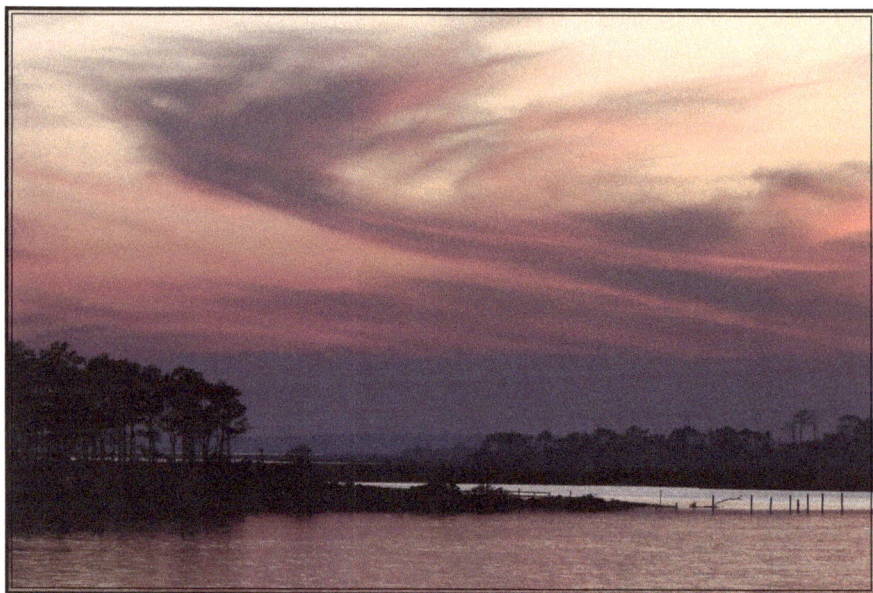

One Man's Imagining

Undulant clouds and purple skies, as the day arrived begins to dim.
The daily work of Earth—the burgeoning, the withering, the blooming again—
now in repose. Until the frost turns morning into sunlit dew.

The solitude of those who witness it, like irises in full bloom, so intimate, the
interfusing of serenity as darkness nears, and the white-yellow moon soon takes its
place, and the scene turns monochrome, we will have our memories of this.

A photograph of one man's imagining, never to be lost again.

The Lighthouse for Our Years

Old days passed, yet the lightkeepers of our lives are still there.
      For every sundown, there is light,
           beams that still shine brightly where we dwell.

Like the lightkeepers, the tides of friends oversee how we are,
      unsaid in part for just being there.

For these are the lightkeepers' shores,
           beyond the times of tides that have rolled in,
      over what has been, and what may still be.
   We still have dreams that harbor us
past the darkness to new light
           just out there.

Misty Eyes

Misty eyes,
　　　　the sea reminds us of those days,
　　we are not ourselves.

Dreaming and waking,
　　　　　　we can feel the stride of the tide
　　　come and go.

We listen to its faint song,
　　　　the *swish* of waves breaking on the shore.

It is a reminder of those we've lost,
sad sounds of our past.

The sea is a silencer of words.
　　　"Be still. Just listen," it says.

It is but a passage for our moods.
　　Even as the mist may hide the way we feel,
it draws us in, like a hug to say,
　　　　　　　"It's alright."

What Heaven Must Be Like

The presence of divinity in its yellow flesh.
All our designs of reality, thoughts and concerns,
mind and body lead us here.

Amidst the aged forest, where the air of brightness glows,
its nightly lastingness goes on and on.

A boy, with phantoms past from an early unseemly world,
grows into a man turned eightyish, beyond his early fate.

His assent, never-ending rebirth of peace, serenity;
it is all there in the yellow glow of godliness,
in the yellow glow of what Heaven must be like.

There Is Only This
(The Last of Humanity)

The wild dog calls; no one answers but the moon.
The hour speaks in darkness through the trees.

The wind wills leaves to shed.

In millennia, rivers change course among
abandoned bluffs.

Otherwise, no sounds of progress bred.
The lure of memory, dim.

Meaninglessness, the ghost of deities.

There is only this: the last human waves goodbye.
There is nothing left to give; nothing left to take.

www.ingramcontent.com/pod-product-compliance
Lightning Source LLC
Chambersburg PA
CBHW041923090426

42741CB00020B/3465